S E L E C T E D

P O

—

WORKS IN ENGLISH BY
CZESLAW MILOSZ

The Captive Mind
Seizure of Power
Postwar Polish Poetry: An Anthology
Native Realm: A Search for Self-Definition
Selected Poems by Zbigniew Herbert
(co-translator)
The History of Polish Literature
Selected Poems
Mediterranean Poems by Aleksander Wat
(translator)
Emperor of the Earth: Modes of Eccentric Vision
Bells in Winter
The Witness of Poetry
The Issa Valley
Visions of San Francisco Bay
The Separate Notebooks
The Land of Ulro
Unattainable Earth
The Collected Poems 1931–1987
With the Skin: Poems of Aleksander Wat
(co-translator)
Happy as a Dog's Tail: Poems by Anna Swir
(co-translator)
Provinces
Beginning with My Streets: Essays and Recollections
A Year of a Hunter
Facing the River: New Poems

Czeslaw Milosz

SELECTED

POEMS

The Ecco Press

To Janka

THE ECCO PRESS
100 West Broad Street
Hopewell, New Jersey 08525
Published simultaneously in Canada by
Penguin Books Canada Ltd., Ontario
Printed in the United States of America
Library of Congress Cataloging-in-Publication Data
Milosz, Czeslaw   /   Selected Poems
PG7158.M553A27 1981   891.8'517   80-21470
ISBN 0-88001-455-5 (paperback)
9 8 7 6

Contents

4

1

A TASK

In fear and trembling, I think I would fulfill my life
Only if I brought myself to make a public confession
Revealing a sham, my own and of my epoch:
We were permitted to shriek in the tongue of dwarfs and
    demons
But pure and generous words were forbidden
Under so stiff a penalty that whoever dared to pronounce one
Considered himself as a lost man.

SHOULD, SHOULD NOT

A man should not love the moon.
An axe should not lose weight in his hand.
His garden should smell of rotting apples
And grow a fair amount of nettles.
A man when he talks should not use words that are dear
    to him,
Or split open a seed to find out what is inside it.
He should not drop a crumb of bread, or spit in the fire
(So at least I was taught in Lithuania).
When he steps on marble stairs,
He may, that boor, try to chip them with his boot
As a reminder that the stairs will not last forever.

LESSONS

Since that moment when in a house with low eaves
A doctor from the town cut the navel-string
And pears dotted with white mildew
Reposed in their nests of luxuriant weeds
I have been in the hands of humans. They could have
    strangled
My first scream, squeezed with a giant hand
The defenseless throat that aroused their tenderness.

From them I received the names of plants and birds,
I lived in their country that was not too barren,
Not too cultivated, with a field, a meadow
And water in a boat moored behind a shed.

Their lessons met, it is true, with a barrier
Deep in myself and my will was dark,
Not very compliant with their intents or mine.
Others, whom I did not know or knew only by name
Were pacing in me and I, terrified,
Heard, in myself, locked creaky rooms
That one should not peep into through a keyhole.
They did not mean much to me—Kazimir, Hrehory
Or Emilia or Margareta.
But I had to repeat all by myself
Every flaw and sin of theirs. This humiliated me.
So that I wanted to shout: you are to blame
For my not being what I want and being what I am.

Sunlight would fall in my book upon Original Sin.
And more than once, when noon was humming in the grass
I would imagine the two of them, with my guilt,
Trampling a wasp beneath the apple tree in Eden.

GREEK PORTRAIT

My beard is thick, my eyelids half cover
My eyes, as with those who know the value
Of visible things. I keep quiet as is proper
For a man who has learned that the human heart
Holds more than speech does. I have left behind
My native land, home and public office.
Not that I looked for profit or adventure.
I am no foreigner on board a ship.
My plain face, the face of a tax-collector,
Merchant, or soldier, makes me one of the crowd.
Nor do I refuse to pay due homage
To local gods. And I eat what others eat.
About myself, this much will suffice.

HAPPINESS

How warm the light! From the glowing bay
The masts, like spruce, repose of the ropes
In the morning mist. Where a stream trickles
Into the sea, by a small bridge—a flute.
Farther, under the arch of ancient ruins
You see a few tiny walking figures.
One wears a red kerchief. There are trees,
Ramparts and mountains at an early hour.

MAGPIETY

The same and not quite the same, I walked through oak
      forests
Amazed that my Muse, Mnemosyne,
Has in no way diminished my amazement.
A magpie was screeching and I said: Magpiety?
What is magpiety? I shall never achieve
A magpie heart, a hairy nostril over the beak, a flight
That always renews just when coming down,
And so I shall never comprehend magpiety.
If however magpiety does not exist
My nature does not exist either.
Who would have guessed that, centuries later,
I would invent the question of universals?

SENTENCES

* * *

What constitutes the training of the hand?
I shall tell what constitutes the training of the hand.
One suspects something is wrong with transcribing signs
But the hand transcribes only the signs it has learned.
Then it is sent to the school of blots and scrawls
Till it forgets what is graceful. For even the sign of a butterfly
Is a well with a coiled poisonous smoke inside.

* * *

Perhaps we should have represented him otherwise
Than in the form of dove. As fire, yes, but that is beyond us.
For even when it consumes logs on a hearth
We search in it for eyes and hands. Let him then be green,
All blades of calamus, running on footbridges
Over meadows, with a thump of his bare feet. Or in the air
Blowing a birchbark trumpet so strongly that further down
There tumbles from its blast a crowd of petty officials,
Their uniforms unbuttoned and their women's combs
Flying like chips when the axe strikes.

* * *

Still it's just too great a responsibility to lure the souls
From where they lived attentive to the idea of the
        hummingbird, the chair and the star.
To imprison them within either-or: male sex, female sex,
So that they wake up in the blood of childbirth, crying.

THESIS AND COUNTER-THESIS

—Love of God is love of self.
The stars and the seas are filled by precious *I*
Sweet as a pillow and a sucked thumb.

—It would be most unflattering for adoring men
If the grasshopper chirping in the warm grass
Could glorify that attribute called *Being*
In a general manner, without referring it to his own persona.

WHAT DOES IT MEAN

It does not know it glitters
It does not know it flies
It does not know it is this not that.

And, more and more often, agape,
With my Gauloise dying out,
Over a glass of red wine,
I muse on the meaning of being this not that.

Just as long ago, when I was twenty,
But then there was a hope I would be everything,
Perhaps even a butterfly or a thrush, by magic.
Now I see dusty district roads
And a town where the postmaster gets drunk every day
Melancholy with remaining identical to himself.

If only the stars contained me.
If only everything kept happening in such a way
That the so-called world opposed the so-called flesh.
Were I at least not contradictory. Alas.

MITTELBERGHEIM

Wine sleeps in casks of Rhine oak.
I am wakened by the bell of a chapel in the vineyards
Of Mittelbergheim. I hear a small spring
Trickling into a well in the yard, a clatter
Of sabots in the street. Tobacco drying
Under the eaves, and ploughs and wooden wheels
And mountain slopes and autumn are with me.

I keep my eyes closed. Do not rush me,
You, fire, power, might, for it is too early.
I have lived through many years and, as in this half-dream,
I felt I was attaining the moving frontier
Beyond which color and sound come true
And the things of this earth are united.
Do not yet force me to open my lips.
Let me trust and believe I will attain.
Let me linger here in Mittelbergheim.

I know I should. They are with me,
Autumn and wooden wheels and tobacco hung
Under the eaves. Here and everywhere
Is my homeland, wherever I turn
And in whatever language I would hear
The song of a child, the conversation of lovers.
Happier than anyone, I am to receive
A glance, a smile, a star, silk creased
At the knee. Serene, beholding,
I am to walk on hills in the soft glow of day
Over waters, cities, roads, human customs.

Fire, power, might, you who hold me
In the palm of your hand whose furrows
Are like immense gorges combed
By southern wind. You who grant certainty
In the hour of fear, in the week of doubt,
It is too early, let the wine mature,
Let the travelers sleep in Mittelbergheim.

KING POPIEL

*Popiel, a legendary king of Polish
prehistory, is said to have been
eaten by mice on his island in the
middle of a big lake.*

Those were not, it is certain, crimes just like ours.
It was all about dugouts carved out of linden trunks
And some beavers' pelts. He ruled over marshes
Where the moose echoes in a moon of acid frosts
And lynxes walk in springtime onto the drying holms.

His palisade, his timber fort and the tower
Built by the fins of the gods of night
Could be seen beyond the water by the hidden hunter
Who dared not push aside the branches with his bow.
Until one of them returned with the news. Over the deep into
     the rushes
The wind chased the largest boat, and it was empty.

Mice have eaten Popiel. The diamond-studded crown
He got later. And to him, who vanished forever,
Who kept in his treasury three Gothic coins
And bars of bronze, to him who went away,
No one knows where, with his children and women,
To him lands and seas were left by Galileo,
Newton and Einstein. So that for long centuries
He might smooth, on his throne, his javelin with a knife.

NO MORE

I should relate sometime how I changed
My views on poetry, and how it came to be
That I consider myself today one of the many
Merchants and artisans of Old Japan,
Who arranged verses about cherry blossoms,
Chrysanthemums and the full moon.

If only I could describe the courtesans of Venice
As in a loggia they teased a peacock with a twig,
And out of brocade, the pearls of their belt,
Set free heavy breasts and the reddish weal
Where the buttoned dress marked the belly,
As vividly as seen by the skipper of galleons
Who landed that morning with a cargo of gold;
And if I could find for their miserable bones
In a graveyard whose gates are licked by greasy water
A word more enduring than their last-used comb
That in the rot under tombstones, alone, awaits the light,

Then I wouldn't doubt. Out of reluctant matter
What can be gathered? Nothing, beauty at best.
And so, cherry blossoms must suffice for us
And chrysanthemums and the full moon.

RIVERS GROW SMALL

Rivers grow small. Cities grow small. And splendid gardens
show what we did not see there before: crippled leaves and
    dust.
When for the first time I swam across the lake
it seemed immense, had I gone there these days
it would have been a shaving bowl
between post-glacial rocks and junipers.
The forest near the village of Halina once was for me primeval
smelling of the last but recently killed bear,
though a ploughed field was visible through the pines.
What was individual becomes a variety of a general pattern.
Consciousness even in my sleep changes primary colors.
The features of my face melt like a wax doll in the fire.
And who can consent to see in the mirror the mere face of
    man?

TO RAJA RAO

Raja, I wish I knew
the cause of that malady.

For years I could not accept
the place I was in.
I felt I should be somewhere else.

A city, trees, human voices
lacked the quality of presence.
I would live by the hope of moving on.

Somewhere else there was a city of real presence,
of real trees and voices and friendship and love.

Link, if you wish, my peculiar case
(on the border of schizophrenia)
to the messianic hope
of my civilization.

Ill at ease in the tyranny, ill at ease in the republic,
in the one I longed for freedom, in the other for the end of
    corruption.

Building in my mind a permanent *polis*
for ever deprived of aimless bustle.

I learned at last to say: this is my home,
here, before the glowing coal of ocean sunsets,
on the shore which faces the shores of your Asia,
in a great republic, moderately corrupt.

Raja, this did not cure me
of my guilt and shame.
A shame of failing to be
what I should have been.

The image of myself
grows gigantic on the wall
and against it
my miserable shadow.

That's how I came to believe
in Original Sin
which is nothing but the first
victory of the ego.

Tormented by my ego, deluded by it
I give you, as you see, a ready argument.

I hear you saying that liberation is possible
and that Socratic wisdom
is identical with your guru's.

No, Raja, I must start from what I am.
I am those monsters which visit my dreams
and reveal to me my hidden essence.

If I am sick, there is no proof whatsoever
that man is a healthy creature.

Greece had to lose, her pure consciousness
had to make our agony only more acute.

We needed God loving us in our weakness
and not in the glory of beatitude.

No help, Raja, my part is agony,
struggle, abjection, self-love and self-hate,
prayer for the Kingdom
and reading Pascal.

AND THE CITY STOOD IN ITS BRIGHTNESS

And the city stood in its brightness when years later I
    returned.
And life was running out, Ruteboeuf's or Villon's.
Descendants, already born, were dancing their dances.
Women looked in their mirrors made from a new metal.
What was it all for if I cannot speak.
She stood above me, heavy, like the earth on its axis.
My ashes were laid in a can under the bistro counter.

And the city stood in its brightness when years later I
    returned
To my home in the display-case of a granite museum,
Beside eyelash mascara, alabaster vials,
And menstruation girdles of an Egyptian princess.
There was only a sun forged out of gold plate,
On darkening parquetry the creak of unhurried steps.

And the city stood in its brightness when years later I
    returned,
My face covered with a coat though now no one was left
Of those who could have remembered my debts never paid,
My shames not forever, base deeds to be forgiven.
And the city stood in its brightness when years later I
    returned.

2

How Once He Was

HYMN

There is no one between you and me.
Neither a plant drawing sap from the depths of earth
nor an animal, nor a man,
nor a wind walking between the clouds.

The most beautiful bodies are like transparent glass.
The most powerful flames like water washing the tired feet
    of travelers.
The greenest trees like lead blooming in the thick of the
    night.
Love is a sand swallowed by parched lips.
Hatred is a salty jug offered to the thirsty.
Roll on, rivers; raise your hands,
cities! I, a faithful son of the black earth, shall return to the
    black earth,
as if my life had not been,
as if not my heart, not my blood,
not my duration
had created words and songs
but an unknown, impersonal voice,
only the flapping of waves, only the choir of winds
and the autumnal sway
of the tall trees.

There is no one between you and me
and to me strength is given.
White mountains graze on terrestrial plains,
to the sea they go, their watering place,
new and new, suns lean over
a valley of a small, dark river where I was born.

I have no wisdom, no skills, and no faith
but I received strength, it tears the world apart.
I shall break, a heavy wave, against its shores
and a young wave will cover my trace. O darkness!
Tainted by the first glare of the dawn,
like a lung taken out of a ripped-up beast,
you are rocking, you are sinking.
How many times I have floated with you,
transfixed in the middle of the night,
hearing some voice above your horror-stricken church;
a cry of grouse, a rustle of the heath were stalking in you
and two apples shone on the table
or open scissors glittered—
and we were alike:
apples, scissors, darkness and I
under the same immobile
Assyrian, Egyptian and Roman
moon.

Seasons come and go, men and women mate,
children in half-sleep run their hands across the wall
and draw lands with a finger wet with saliva.
Forms come and go, what seemed invincible, crumbles.

But amid the States rising from the sea,
amid demolished streets where one day
mountains will loom made of a fallen planet,
against what is past and what is to pass
youth defends itself, austere as the sundust,
in love neither with good nor with evil,
all tossed under your immense feet,
so that you may crush it, so that you may step on it,
so that your breath move the wheel
and a frail structure shake with motion,

so that you give to it hunger and to others wine, salt and
   bread.

The sound of the horn still is not heard
calling the dispersed, those who lie in the valleys.
On the frozen ground as yet no rumble of the last cart.
There is no one between you and me.

1934.

STATUE OF A COUPLE

Your hand, my wonder, is now icy cold.
The purest light of the celestial dome
has burned me through. And now we are
as two still plains lying in darkness,
as two black banks of a frozen stream
in the chasm of the world.

Our hair combed back is carved in wood,
the moon walks over our ebony shoulders.
A distant cockcrow, the night goes by, silent.
Rich is the rime of love, withered the dowry.

Where are you, living in what depths of time,
love, stepping down into what waters,
now, when the frost of our voiceless lips
does not fend off the divine fires?

In a forest of clouds, of foam and of silver
we live, caressing lands under our feet.
And we are wielding the might of a dark scepter
to earn oblivion.

My love, your breast cut through by a chisel
knows nothing any more of what it was.
Of clouds at dawn, of angers at daybreak,
of shadows in springtime it has no remembrance.

And you have led me, as once an angel led
Tobias, onto the rusty marshes of Lombardy.
But a day came when a sign frightened you,
a stigma of golden measure.

With a scream, with immobile fear in your thin hands
you fell into a pit that ashes lie over,
where neither northern firs nor Italian yews
could protect our ancient bed of lovers.

What was it, what is it, what will it be—
we filled the world with our cry and calling.
The dawn is back, the red moon set,
do we know now? In a heavy ship

A helmsman comes, throws a silken rope
and binds us tightly to each other,
then he pours on friends, once enemies,
a handful of snow.

1935.

39

DAY OF GENERATION

When, once entangled in motions of their legs,
Cyclists on the highway lean at a curve,
In the air that is childish, rosy
And all prepared for other shapes,
For an outline of non-mortal feet,

When, clipping through the mist with glints of their legs,
They enter in the morning some human city,
And sunflowers of outskirts dash over the haze
And the poplar phantoms lilt in space,

A peasant woman bent under her basket,
Walking at dawn, cuts across the crowd
Of invisible dwellers whose towering chambers
Are not to be discovered by her eye.

      * * *

It's enough to raise your hand to touch
Somebody's cheek, to find a satin dress,
To recognize a smile of ancient days,
A foam-like chain, a shell-incrusted comb.

A wizard, taking a wand or a chisel,
Will call: *Let it be,* bring forth from the air
A carriage and four in immobile speed
Or a bronze forearm punctured by the rains.

And where there was a circle of white void
Now little reddish flames are running to and fro.
So much that air got thick by being touched,

Layer after layer changed into waterfalls.
They turn, the helices of stone-hard flowers,
The whole earth smells of lightnings as in spring.
A wand, a chisel falls from your hands. Perish.

Too late. An unrestrained chorus pushes on.
Ranks of reed-pipes, of adroit fingers.
The smoke of banners claps right over them.
Abysses have been hit and now fade out.
For the sake of history small as a plaything,
To the doom of wizards as sad as fate.
And monuments wet with dew will shine on the squares.

                *   *   *

Then glints of legs clip through the break of day,
There is also a peasant woman with her basket
And sunflowers sway over the haze.
Now somebody else calls you in,
Now somebody else summons you
Where you are both a self and not a self.

        ENVOY

It is your destiny so to move your wand,
To wake up storms, to run through the heart of storms,
To lay bare a monument like a nest in a thicket,
Though all you wanted was to pluck a few roses.

3

What Did He Learn

DEDICATION

You whom I could not save
Listen to me.
Try to understand this simple speech as I would be ashamed
   of another.
I swear, there is in me no wizardry of words.
I speak to you with silence like a cloud or a tree.

What strengthened me, for you was lethal.
You mixed up farewell to an epoch with the beginning of a
   new one,
Inspiration of hatred with lyrical beauty,
Blind force with accomplished shape.

Here is the valley of shallow Polish rivers. And an immense
   bridge
Going into white fog. Here is a broken city,
And the wind throws the screams of gulls on your grave
When I am talking with you.

What is poetry which does not save
Nations or people?
A connivance with official lies,
A song of drunkards whose throats will be cut in a moment,
Readings for sophomore girls.
That I wanted good poetry without knowing it,
That I discovered, late, its salutary aim,
In this and only this I find salvation.

They used to pour millet on graves or poppy seeds
To feed the dead who would come disguised as birds.

I put this book here for you, who once lived
So that you should visit us no more.

Warsaw, 1945.

SONG OF A CITIZEN

A stone deep below who has witnessed the seas drying up
and a million white fish leaping in agony,
I, poor man, see a multitude of white-bellied nations
without freedom. I see the crab feeding on their flesh.

I have seen the fall of States and the perdition of tribes,
the flight of kings and emperors, the power of tyrants.
I can say now, in this hour,
that I—am, while everything expires,
that it is better to be a live dog than a dead lion
as the Scripture says.

A poor man, sitting on a cold chair, pressing my eyelids,
I sigh and think of a starry sky,
of non-Euclidean space, of amoebas and their pseudopodia,
of tall mounds of termites.

When walking, I am asleep, when sleeping, I dream reality,
pursued and covered with sweat, I run.
On city squares lifted up by the glaring dawn,
beneath marble remnants of blasted-down gates,
I deal in vodka and gold.

And yet so often I was near,
I reached into the heart of metal, the soul of earth, of fire,
     of water.
And the unknown unveiled its face
as a night reveals itself, serene, mirrored by tide.
Lustrous copper-leaved gardens greeted me
that disappear as soon as you touch them.

And so near, just outside the window—the greenhouse of the
    worlds
where a tiny beetle and a spider are equal to planets,
where a wandering atom flares up like Saturn,
and, close by, harvesters drink from a cold jug
in scorching summer.

This I wanted and nothing more. In my later years
like old Goethe to stand before the face of the earth,
and recognize it and reconcile it
with my work built up, a forest citadel
on a river of shifting lights and brief shadows.

This I wanted and nothing more. So who
is guilty? Who deprived me
of my youth and my ripe years, who seasoned
my best years with horror? Who,
who ever is to blame, who, O God?

And I can think only about the starry sky,
about the tall mounds of termites.

                                    Warsaw, 1942.

A POOR CHRISTIAN LOOKS AT THE GHETTO

Bees build around red liver,
Ants build around black bone.
It has begun: the tearing, the trampling on silks,
It has begun: the breaking of glass, wood, copper, nickel,
    silver, foam
Of gypsum, iron sheets, violin strings, trumpets, leaves, balls,
    crystals.
Poof! Phosphorescent fire from yellow walls
Engulfs animal and human hair.

Bees build around the honeycomb of lungs,
Ants build around white bone.
Torn is paper, rubber, linen, leather, flax,
Fiber, fabrics, cellulose, snakeskin, wire.
The roof and the wall collapse in flame and heat seizes the
    foundations.
Now there is only the earth, sandy, trodden down,
With one leafless tree.

Slowly, boring a tunnel, a guardian mole makes his way,
With a small red lamp fastened to his forehead.
He touches buried bodies, counts them, pushes on,
He distinguishes human ashes by their luminous vapor,
The ashes of each man by a different part of the spectrum.
Bees build around a red trace.
Ants build around the place left by my body.

I am afraid, so afraid of the guardian mole.
He has swollen eyelids, like a Patriarch
Who has sat much in the light of candles
Reading the great book of the species.

What will I tell him, I, a Jew of the New Testament,
Waiting two thousand years for the second coming of Jesus?
My broken body will deliver me to his sight
And he will count me among the helpers of death:
The uncircumcised.

Warsaw, 1943.

CAFE

Of that table in the café
where on winter noons a garden of frost glittered on window
    panes
I survived alone.
I could go in there if I wanted to
and drumming my fingers in a chilly void
convoke shadows.

With disbelief I touch the cold marble,
with disbelief I touch my own hand.
It—is, and I—am in ever novel becoming,
while they are locked forever and ever
in their last word, their last glance,
and as remote as Emperor Valentinian
or the chiefs of the Massagetes, about whom I know nothing,
though hardly one year has passed, or two or three.

I may still cut trees in the woods of the far North,
I may speak from a platform or shoot a film
using techniques they never heard of.
I may learn the taste of fruits from ocean islands
and be photographed in an attire from the second half of the
    century.
But they are forever like busts in frock coats and jabots
in some monstrous encyclopedia.

Sometimes when the evening aurora paints the roofs in a
    poor street
and I contemplate the sky, I see in the white clouds
a table wobbling. The waiter whirls with his tray

and they look at me with a burst of laughter
for I still don't know what it is to die at the hand of man,
they know—they know it well.

Warsaw, 1944.

THE POOR POET

The first movement is singing,
A free voice, filling mountains and valleys.
The first movement is joy,
But it is taken away.

And now that the years have transformed my blood
And thousands of planetary systems have been born and died
    in my flesh,
I sit, a sly and angry poet
With malevolently squinted eyes,
And, weighing a pen in my hand,
I plot revenge.

I poise the pen and it puts forth twigs and leaves, it is covered
    with blossoms
And the scent of that tree is impudent, for there, on the real
    earth,
Such trees do not grow, and like an insult
To suffering humanity is the scent of that tree.

Some take refuge in despair, which is sweet
Like strong tobacco, like a glass of vodka drunk in the hour
    of annihilation.
Others have the hope of fools, rosy as erotic dreams.

Still others find peace in the idolatry of country,
Which can last for a long time,
Although little longer than the nineteenth century lasts.

But to me a cynical hope is given,
For since I opened my eyes I have seen only the glow of fires,
    massacres,

Only injustice, humiliation, and the laughable shame of
    braggarts.
To me is given the hope of revenge on others and on myself,
For I was he who knew
And took from it no profit for myself.

Warsaw, 1944.

OUTSKIRTS

A hand with cards drops down
on the hot sand.
The sun turned white drops down
on the hot sand.
Ted holds the bank. Ted is now dealing.
The glare stabs through the sticky pack
into hot sand.

A broken shadow of a chimney. Thin grass.
Farther on, the city opened with red brick.
Brown heaps, barbed-wire tangled at stations.
Dry rib of a rusty automobile.
A claypit glitters.

An empty bottle buried
in the hot sand.
A drop of rain raised dust
off the hot sand.
Jack holds the bank. Jack is now dealing.
We play, Julys and Mays go by.
We play one year, we play a fourth.
The glare pours through our blackened cards
into hot sand.

Farther on, the city opened with red brick.
A lone pine-tree behind a Jewish house.
Loose footprints and the plain up to the horizon.
A lime fall-out, wagons are rolling,
and in the wagons a whining lament.

Take a mandolin, on the mandolin
you'll play it all.
Hey, fingers, strings.
So nice a song.
A barren field.
The glass tossed off.
No more is needed.

Look, there she goes, a pretty girl.
Cork-soled slippers and curly hair.
Hello sweetheart, let's have a good time.
A barren field.
The sun is setting.

Warsaw, 1944.

A SONG ON THE END OF THE WORLD

On the day the world ends
A bee circles a clover,
A fisherman mends a glimmering net.
Happy porpoises jump in the sea,
By the rainspout young sparrows are playing
And the snake is gold-skinned as it should always be.

On the day the world ends
Women walk through the fields under their umbrellas,
A drunkard grows sleepy at the edge of a lawn,
Vegetable peddlers shout in the street
And a yellow-sailed boat comes nearer the island,
The voice of a violin lasts in the air
And leads into a starry night.

And those who expected lightning and thunder
Are disappointed.
And those who expected signs and archangels' trumps
Do not believe it is happening now.
As long as the sun and the moon are above,
As long as the bumblebee visits a rose,
As long as rosy infants are born
No one believes it is happening now.

Only a white-haired old man, who would be a prophet
Yet is not a prophet, for he's much too busy,
Repeats while he binds his tomatoes:
There will be no other end of the world,
There will be no other end of the world.

Warsaw, 1944.

MID-TWENTIETH-CENTURY PORTRAIT

Hidden behind his smile of brotherly regard,
He despises the newspaper reader, the victim of the dialectic
    of power.
Says: "Democracy," with a wink.
Hates the physiological pleasures of mankind,
Full of memories of those who also ate, drank, copulated,
But in a moment had their throats cut.
Recommends dances and garden parties to defuse public
    anger.

Shouts: "Culture!" and "Art!", but means circus games really.

Utterly spent.
Mumbles in sleep or anaesthesia: "God, oh God!"
Compares himself to a Roman in whom the Mithra cult has
    mixed with the cult of Jesus.
Still clings to old superstitions, sometimes believes himself to
    be possessed by demons.
Attacks the past, but fears that, having destroyed it,
He will have nothing on which to lay his head.
Likes most to play cards, or chess, the better to keep his own
    counsel.

Keeping one hand on Marx's writings, he reads the Bible in
    private.
His mocking eye on processions leaving burnt-out churches.
His backdrop: a horseflesh-colored city in ruins.
In his hand: a memento of a boy "fascist" killed in the
    Uprising.

Cracow, 1945.

CHILD OF EUROPE

1

We, whose lungs fill with the sweetness of day,
Who in May admire trees flowering,
Are better than those who perished.

We, who taste of exotic dishes,
And enjoy fully the delights of love,
Are better than those who were buried.

We, from the fiery furnaces, from behind barbed wires
On which the winds of endless Autumns howled,
We, who remember battles where the wounded air roared
     in paroxysms of pain,
We, saved by our own cunning and knowledge.

By sending others to the more exposed positions,
Urging them loudly to fight on,
Ourselves withdrawing in certainty of the cause lost.

Having the choice of our own death and that of a friend,
We chose his, coldly thinking: let it be done quickly.

We sealed gas chamber doors, stole bread,
Knowing the next day would be harder to bear than the day
     before.

As befits human beings, we explored good and evil.
Our malignant wisdom has no like on this planet.

Accept it as proven that we are better than they,
The gullible, hot-blooded weaklings, careless with their lives.

2

Treasure your legacy of skills, child of Europe,
Inheritor of gothic cathedrals, of baroque churches,
Of synagogues filled with the wailing of a wronged people.
Successor of Descartes, Spinoza, inheritor of the word
    "honor,"
Posthumous child of Leonidas,
Treasure the skills acquired in the hour of terror.

You have a clever mind which sees instantly
The good and bad of any situation.
You have an elegant, skeptical mind which enjoys pleasures
Quite unknown to primitive races.

Guided by this mind you cannot fail to see
The soundness of the advice we give you:
Let the sweetness of day fill your lungs.
For this we have strict but wise rules.

3

There can be no question of force triumphant.
We live in the age of victorious justice.

Do not mention force, or you will be accused
Of upholding fallen doctrines in secret.

He who has power, has it by historical logic.
Respectfully bow to that logic.

Let your lips, proposing a hypothesis,
Not know about the hand faking the experiment.

Let your hand, faking the experiment,
Not know about the lips proposing a hypothesis.

Learn to predict a fire with unerring precision.
Then burn the house down to fulfill the prediction.

4

Grow your tree of falsehood from a small grain of truth.
Do not follow those who lie in contempt of reality.

Let your lie be even more logical than the truth itself,
So the weary travelers may find repose in the lie.

After the Day of the Lie gather in select circles,
Shaking with laughter when our real deeds are mentioned.

Dispensing flattery called: perspicacious thinking.
Dispensing flattery called: a great talent.

We, the last who can still draw joy from cynicism.
We, whose cunning is not unlike despair.

A new, humorless generation is now arising,
It takes in deadly earnest all we received with laughter.

5

Let your words speak not through their meanings,
But through them against whom they are used.

Fashion your weapon from ambiguous words.
Consign clear words to lexical limbo.

Judge no words before the clerks have checked
In their card index by whom they were spoken.

The voice of passion is better than the voice of reason.
The passionless cannot change history.

6

Love no country: countries soon disappear.
Love no city: cities are soon rubble.

Throw away keepsakes, or from your desk
A choking, poisonous fume will exude.

Do not love people: people soon perish.
Or they are wronged and call for your help.

Do not gaze into the pools of the past.
Their corroded surface will mirror
A face different from the one you expected.

7

He who invokes history is always secure.
The dead will not rise to witness against him.

You can accuse them of any deeds you like.
Their reply will always be silence.

Their empty faces swim out of the deep dark.
You can fill them with any features desired.

Proud of dominion over people long vanished,
Change the past into your own, better likeness.

8

The laughter born of the love of truth
Is now the laughter of the enemies of the people.

Gone is the age of satire. We no longer need mock
The senile tyrant with false courtly phrases.

Stern as befits the servants of a cause,
We will permit ourselves only sycophantic humor.

Tight-lipped, guided by reasons only,
Cautiously let us step into the era of the unchained fire.

RECOVERY

*(From "The World," poem in a
primer's rhyme)*

Here I am—why this unreasonable fear?
Soon night will go away, the day will rise.
Listen: already shepherds' horns are
Playing. The stars fade over a red trace.

The Path is straight: we are on the edge.
A bell rings below in the village
And roosters on the fences are welcoming
Light; the earth, fertile and happy, steams.

Here it is still dark. Like a flooded river
Fog envelops the black tuffets of huckleberries.
But already the dawn on stilts enters water,
And the sunny ball ringing rolls.

THE SPIRIT OF THE LAWS

From the cry of children on the floors of stations beyond time,
From the sadness of the engineer of prison trains,
From the red scars of two wars on the forehead
I awoke under the bronze of winged monuments,
Under the griffins of a Masonic temple
With the dying ash of a cigar.

It was a summer of plane trees in colonnades and pearls of
    birds poured from the dawn,
A summer of joined hands, of black, of violet,
A summer of blue bees, of whistles, of flames
And the tiny propellers of a hummingbird.

And I, with my pine anchor on a sandy plain,
With the silenced memory of dead friends
And the silenced memory of towns and rivers,
I was ready to tear out the heart of the earth with a knife
And put there a glowing diamond of shouts and complaints,
I was ready to smear the bottom of roots with blood
To invoke the names on their leaves,
To cover the malachite of monuments with the skin of night
And write down with phosphorus Mene Tekel Upharsin,
Shining with the traces of melting eyelids.

I could go to the riverside where lovers
Look at the remnants of games floating to the sea,
I could enter parking lots, iridescent soap bubbles
And listen to the laboring
Of the eternal humanity of muted notes,
Of industrious, agile male muscles
Over a hot butterfly of carmine.

Gardens hopping down to the bottom of ravines,
The national dances of gray squirrels
And the white laboratories of winged infants
Always growing up in a different epoch,
The shine, the juice, the rouge of the day
All of it
Seemed to be the beginning of the sun on yellow plains
Where in railway stations at a wobbling table,
Sitting over an empty glass, their faces in their hands,
Are the sad engineers of prison trains.

1947.

BIRTH

For the first time he sees light.
The world is garish light.
He doesn't know these are shrieks
Of garish birds.
Their hearts beat quickly
Under enormous leaves.
He doesn't know birds live
In another time than man.
He doesn't know a tree lives
In another time than birds
And will grow slowly
Upwards in a grey column
Thinking with its roots
Of the silver of underworld kingdoms.

The last of the tribe, he comes
After great magic dances.
After the dance of the Antelope,
After the dance of the Winged Snakes
Under an eternally blue sky
In a valley of brick-red mountains.

He comes after spotted thongs
On a shield with a monster's face,
After deities who send down
Dreams by their painted eyelid,
After the rust of carved ships
Which the wind has forgotten.

He comes, after grating of swords
And voice of battle horns,

After the weird mass shriek
In the dust of shattered brick
After the flutter of fans
Over a joke of warm teacups,
After swan lake dances,
And after a steam engine.

Wherever he steps, there always
Endures traced in sand
A large-toed footprint
Which clamors to be tried out
By his childish foot arriving
Out of the virgin forests.

Wherever he goes, he always
Will find on things of the earth,
A warm luster furbished
By a human hand.
This will never leave him,
It will stay with him always,
A presence close as breath,
His only wealth.

1947.

4

Shore

WHAT ONCE WAS GREAT

To A. and O. Wat

What once was great, now appeared small.
Kingdoms were fading like snow-covered bronze.

What once could smite, now smites no more.
Celestial earths roll on and shine.

Stretched on the grass by the bank of a river,
As long, long ago, I launch my boats of bark.

OCEAN

A gentle tongue lapping
Small chubby knees,
Envoys bringing salt
From a billion-year-old abyss.
Here are violet thistles,
Peached suns of jellyfish,
Here with airplane fins
And skin of graters, sharks
Visit the museum of death
Under water-towers of crystal.
A dolphin shows from a wave
The face of a black boy,
In the liquid cities of the desert
Graze leviathans.

ALBUM OF DREAMS

May 10

Did I mistake the house or the street
or perhaps the staircase, though once I was there every day?
I looked through the keyhole. The kitchen: the same and not
    the same.
And I carried, wound on a reel,
a plastic tape, narrow as a shoelace,
that was everything I had written over the long years.
I rang, uncertain whether I would hear that name.
She stood before me in her saffron dress,
unchanged, greeting me with a smile without one tear of time.
And in the morning chickadees were singing in the cedar.

June 17

And that snow will remain forever,
unredeemed, not spoken of to anyone.
On it their track freezes at sunset
in an hour, in a year, in a district, in a country.

And that face will remain forever
beaten for ages by drops of rain.
One drop is running from eyelid to lip
on an empty square, in an unnamed city.

75

August 14

They ordered us to pack our things, as the house was to be
    burned.
There was time to write a letter, but that letter was with me.
We laid down our bundles and sat against the wall.
They looked when we placed a violin on the bundles.
My little sons did not cry. Gravity and curiosity.
One of the soldiers brought a can of gasoline. Others were
    tearing down curtains.

November 18

He showed us a road which led down.
We would not get lost, he said, there were many lights.
Through abandoned orchards, vineyards and embankments
overgrown with brambles we took a shortcut,
and the lights were, as you will—the lanterns
of gigantic glowworms, or small planets
descending in uncertain flight.
Once, when we tried to make a turn up
everything went out. And in total darkness
I understood we must march on into the gorge
since only then the lights would lead us again.
I held her hand, we were united
by bodily memory
of journeying together on a lovers' bed
that is to say one time in the wheat or a dense forest.
Below a torrent roared, there were frozen rockslides
the atrocious color of lunar sulphur.

November 23

A long train is standing in the station and the platform is
    empty.
Winter, night, the frozen sky is flooded with red.
Only a woman's weeping is heard. She is pleading for
    something
from an officer in a stone coat.

December 1

The halls of the infernal station, drafty and cold.
A knock at the door, the door opens
and my dead father appears in the doorway
but he is young, handsome, beloved.
He offers me his hand. I run away from him
down a spiral staircase, never-ending.

December 3

With a broad white beard and dressed in velvet,
Walt Whitman was leading dances in a country manor
owned by Swedenborg, Emanuel.
And I was there as well, drinking mead and wine.
At first we circled hand in hand
and resembled stones overgrown with mold,
set into motion. Then the invisible
orchestras played more quickly, and we were seized
by the madness of the dance, in elation.
And that dance, of harmony, of concord
was a dance of happy Hassidim.

December 14

I moved my strong wings, below were gliding
bluish meadows, willows, a winding river.
Here is the castle with its moat, and nearby, the gardens
where my beloved takes a walk.
But as I returned, I had to take care
not to lose the magic book
stuck in my belt. I could never manage
to soar very high, and there were mountains.
I struggled painfully to the ridge above the forest
rusty from the leaves of oaks and chestnuts.
There, at birds carved on a dry branch,
an invisible hand was throwing boughs
to draw me down by magic means.
I fell. She kept me on her glove,
now a hawk with bloodstained plume,
the Witch of the Desert. In the castle she had found out
the incantations printed in my book.

March 16

The unsummoned face. How he died no one knows.
I repeated my question until he took flesh.
And he, a boxer, hits the guard in the jaw,
for which boots trample him. I look at the guard
with dog's eyes and have one desire:
to carry out every order, so he will praise me.
And even when he sent me to the city,
a city of arcades, of passages, of marble squares
(it seems to be Venice), stepping on the slabs,
in funny rags, barefoot, with an oversize cap,

I think of fulfilling only what he assigned me,
I show my permits and carry for him
a Japanese doll (the vendor didn't know its value).

March 24

It is a country on the edge of the Rudnicka Wilderness,
for example, beside the sawmill at Yashuny, between the
    fir-forest of Kleyvy
and the villages of Chernitza, Mariampol, Halina.
Perhaps the river Yerres runs there
between banks of anemones on marshy meadows.
The inseminator-pines, footbridges, tall ferns.
How the earth heaves! Not in order to burst,
but it tells with a movement of its skin
that it can make trees bow to one another and tumble down.
For that reason joy. Such as people never
have known before. Rejoice! Rejoice!
in a path, in a shack, in a protruding stone.
And water! But in that water whatever you shoot sinks.
Joseph, smelling of cheap tobacco, stands on the bank.
—I shot a bear, but it fell in. —When?
—This afternoon. —Stupid, look, see that keg?
There's your bear, floating in it. Where's the bear? Shame.
It's only a wounded bear cub breathing.

March 26

Through the meadow fields at night,
through the meadow fields of civilization
we ran shouting, singing, in a tongue not our own
but one which terrified others.

79

They ran before us, we took two-yard,
three-yard strides,
limitlessly powerful, happy.
Turning out its lights, a car stopped: a different one,
a car from there. We heard voices
speaking near us in a tongue we had used only for amusement.
Now we, the pretenders, were seized by fear
so great that over fences and palisades
in fourteen-yard leaps we ran into the depths of the forest.
And behind us the hue and cry
in a Scythian or Lombard dialect.

April 3

Our expedition rode into a land of dry lava.
Perhaps under us were armor and crowns
but here there was not a tree,
or even lichens growing on the rocks,
and in the birdless sky, racing through filmy clouds
the sun went down between black concretions.

When slowly, in that complete stillness
in which not a lizard was rustling
gravel began to crunch under the wheels of the trucks
suddenly we saw, standing on a hill
a pink corset with ribbon floating.
Further a second and a third. So, baring our heads,
we walked towards them, temples in ruins.

THROUGHOUT OUR LANDS

1

When I pass'd through a populous city
(as Walt Whitman says, in the Polish version)
when I pass'd through a populous city,
for instance near San Francisco harbor, counting gulls,
I thought that between men, women, and children there is
something, neither happiness nor unhappiness.

2

At noon white rubble of cemeteries on the hillsides:
a city of eye-dazzling cements
glued together with the slime of winged insects
spins with the sky about the spiraled freeways.

3

If I had to tell what the world is for me
I would take a hamster or a hedgehog or a mole
and place him in a theater seat one evening
and, bringing my ear close to his humid snout,
would listen to what he says about the spotlights,
sounds of the music, and movements of the dance.

4

Was I breaking the sound barrier?
And then clouds with cathedrals,
ecstatic greens beyond wrought-iron gates
and silence, surprisingly, different from what I'd known.
Here I am where the fist of an old woman is wrapped with a
　　　rosary,
a cane taps on flagstones between dappled shadows.
Is it a shame or not
that this is my portion?

5

Waking before dawn, I saw the grey lake
and, as usual, two men trolling in a motorboat, which
　　　sputtered slowly.
Next, I was awakened by the sun shining straight into my eyes
as it stood above the pass on the Nevada side.
Between the moment and the moment 1 lived through much
　　　in my sleep
so distinctly that I felt time dissolve
and knew that what was past still is, not was.
And I hope this will be counted somehow in my defense:
my regret and great longing once to express
one life, not for my glory, for a different splendor.
Later on a slight wind creased the iridescent water.
I was forgetting. Snow glittered on the mountains.

6

And the word revealed out of darkness was: pear.
I hovered around it hopping or trying my wings.
But whenever I was just about to drink its sweetness, it
    withdrew.
So I tried Anjou—then a garden's corner,
scaling white paint of wooden shutters,
a dogwood bush and rustling of departed people.
So I tried Comice—then right away fields
beyond this (not another) palisade, a brook, countryside.
So I tried Jargonelle, Bosc and Bergamot.
No good. Between me and pear, equipages, countries.
And so I have to live, with this spell on me.

7

With their chins high, girls come back from the tennis courts.
The spray rainbows over the sloping lawns.
With short jerks a robin runs up, stands motionless.
The eucalyptus tree trunks glow in the light.
The oaks perfect the shadow of May leaves.
Only this is worthy of praise. Only this: the day.

But beneath it elemental powers are turning somersaults;
and devils, mocking the naive who believe in them,
play catch with hunks of bloody meat,
whistle songs about matter without beginning or end,
and about the moment of our agony
when everything we have cherished will appear
an artifice of cunning self-love.

8

And what if Pascal had not been saved
and if those narrow hands in which we laid a cross
are just he, entire, like a lifeless swallow
in the dust, under the buzz of the poisonous-blue flies?

And if they all, kneeling with poised palms,
millions, billions of them, ended together with their illusion?
I shall never agree. I will give them the crown.
The human mind is splendid; lips powerful,
and the summons so great it must open Paradise.

9

They are so persistent, that give them a few stones
and edible roots, and they will build the world.

10

Over his grave they were playing Mozart
Since they had nothing to keep themselves distinct
From the yellow dirt, clouds, wilted dahlias
And under a sky too big, there was too much silence.

And just as at the tea-party of a princess
When a stalactite of wax drips out the measure,
And a wick sizzles, and shoulders in frock coats
Gleam in their rows of high gold-braided collars,

Mozart has sounded, unwrapped from the powder of wigs,
And suspended on trails of late-summer gossamer
Vanishing overhead, in that void where
A jet has gone, leaving a thin white seam.

While he, a contemporary of no one,
Black as a grub beneath the winter bark,
Was at work already, calling in rust and mold
So as to vanish, before they took the faded wreaths.

11

Paulina, her room behind the servants' quarters, with one
        window on the orchard
where I gather the best apples near the pigsty
squishing with my big toe the warm muck of the dunghill,
and the other window on the well (I love to drop the bucket
        down
and scare its inhabitants, the green frogs).
Paulina, a geranium, the chill of a dirt floor,
a hard bed with three pillows,
an iron crucifix and images of the saints,
decorated with palms and paper roses.
Paulina died long ago, but is.
And, I am somehow convinced, not just in my consciousness.

Above her rough Lithuanian peasant face
hovers a spindle of hummingbirds, and her flat calloused feet
are sprinkled by sapphire water in which dolphins
with their backs arching
frolic.

12

Wherever you are, colors of the sky envelop you
just as here, shrill oranges and violets,
the smell of a leaf pulped in your fingers accompanies you
even in your dream, birds are named
in the language of that place: a *towhee* came to the kitchen,
scatter some bread on the lawn, *juncos* have arrived.
Wherever you are, you touch the bark of trees
testing its roughness different yet familiar.
Grateful for a rising and a setting sun
wherever you are, you could never be an alien.

Was Father Junipero an alien, when on mule-back
he came here, wandering through the deserts of the south.
He found redskin brothers. Their reason and memory
were dimmed. They had been roaming very far
from the Euphrates, the Pamirs, and the heights of Cathay,
slowly, as far as any generation can
pursuing its goal: good hunting grounds.
And there, where later the land sank into the cold
shallow sea, they had lived thousands of years,
until they had almost completely forgotten the Garden of
    Eden
and had not yet learned the reckoning of time.
Father Junipero, born on the Mediterranean
brought them news about their first parents,
about the signs, the promise, and the expectation.
He told them, exiles, that there, in their native land,
their guilt had been washed away, just as dust is washed
from their foreheads, sprinkled with water.
It was like something they had heard of long ago.

But, poor people, they had lost the gift of concentration
and a preacher had to hang from his neck a roasted flank of
      deer
in order to attract their greedy eyes.
But then they slobbered, so loudly, he could not speak.

Nonetheless it was they who in my place took possession
of rocks on which only mute dragons
were basking from the beginning, crawling out of the sea.
They sewed a clock from the plumage of flickers,
      hummingbirds, and tanagers,
and a brown arm, throwing back the mantle, would point to:
      this.
And the land was henceforth conquered: seen.

13

Whiskers of rabbits and downy necks
of yellow-black ducklings, the flowing fire
of a fox in the green, touch the heart
of master and slave. And also musics
starting under the trees. A snare drum, a flute
or a concertina or from a gramophone
the voices of djinns bleating jazz.
A swing goes up to the clouds, and those looking from below
have their breath taken away by the darkness under a skirt.
Who has not dreamt of the Marquis de Sade's *châteaux?*
When one ("ah-h-h!") rubs his hands
and to the job: to gouge with a spur
young girls drawn up in line for footrace
or to order naked nuns in black net stockings
to lash us with a whip as we bite the bedsheets.

14

Cabeza, if anyone knew all about civilization, it was you.
A bookkeeper from Castile, what a fix you were in
to have to wander about, where no notion,
no cipher, no stroke of a pen dipped in sepia,
only a boat thrown up on the sand by surf,
crawling naked on all fours, under the eye of immobile
     Indians,
and suddenly their wail in the void of sky and sea,
their lament: that even the gods are unhappy.
For seven years you were their predicted god,
bearded, white-skinned, beaten if you couldn't work a miracle.
Seven years' march from the Mexican Gulf to California,
the hu-hu-hu of tribes, hot bramble of the continent.
But afterwards? Who am I, the lace of cuffs
not mine, the table carved with lions not mine, Doña Clara's
fan, the slipper from under her gown—hell, no.
On all fours! On all fours!
Smear our thighs with war paint.
Lick the ground. Wha wha, hu hu.

THREE TALKS ON CIVILIZATION

1

The dark blush of anger
the impolite reply
the loathing of foreigners
uphold the State.

Roars at a touchdown
slums near the harbors
liquor for the poor
uphold the State.

Hermance, if at a twist of my ring
those quarters vanished through which my retinue
rushes forward not to see eyes fixed on nothing,

if people (instead of everyday necessity and the, so to speak,
hairy pleasures proper to the flesh)
spick-and-span, pretending they do not stink at all,

nibbled chocolates in a theater,
if they were moved by the loves of Amyntas,
and in the daytime read the *Summa,* luckily too difficult,

none would be fit for the barracks. The State would fall.

2

Yes, it is true that the landscape changed a little.
Where there were forests, now there are pears of factories,
    gas tanks.
Approaching the mouth of the river we hold our noses.
Its current carries oil and chlorine and methyl compounds,
Not to mention the by-products of the Books of Abstraction:
Excrement, urine, and dead sperm.
A huge stain of artificial color poisons fish in the sea.
Where the shore of the bay was overgrown with rushes
Now it is rusted with smashed machines, ashes and bricks.
We used to read in old poets about the scent of earth
And grasshoppers. Now we bypass the fields:
Ride as fast as you can through the chemical zone of the
    farmers.
The insect and the bird are extinguished. Far away a bored
    man
Drags the dust with his tractor, an umbrella against the sun.
What do we regret?—I ask. A tiger? A shark?
We created a second Nature in the image of the first
So as not to believe that we live in Paradise.
It is possible that when Adam woke in the garden
The beasts licked the air and yawned, friendly,
While their fangs and their tails, lashing their backs,
Were figurative and the red-backed shrike,
Later, much later, named *Lanius collurio,*
Did not impale caterpillars on spikes of the blackthorn.
However, other than that moment, what we know of Nature
Does not speak in its favor. Ours is no worse.
So I beg you, no more of those lamentations.

3

If I only knew one thing, this one thing:
Can contrition be just wounded pride?

Wood-paneled corridors open.
A satin slipper patters down a sloping floor.
Dear neck, its scent lingers forever.
Already henchmen come running with proofs of my crime:
Bloodstains in a suburb, the forgotten knife.

And when they chase me on the stairs till dawn,
I cannot tell, stumbling, grasping at curtains,
Whether my terror is perfect remorse,
Or shame of dying without dignity.
Later I stare in the mirror at my swollen eyelids.

Therefore, I think, I wrote to Alexander,
Advising him to curb the youth societies,
(You will find this, Hermantia, dated eighteen twenty).
I detested these pups of foolish Jean-Jacques,
And envied them their belief in their own noble nature.

A MAGIC MOUNTAIN

I sleep a lot and read St. Thomas Aquinas
or *The Death of God* (that's a Protestant book).
To the right the bay as if molten tin,
beyond the bay, city, beyond the city, ocean,
beyond the ocean, ocean, till Japan.
To the left dry hills with white grass,
beyond the hills an irrigated valley where rice is grown,
beyond the valley, mountains and Ponderosa pines,
beyond the mountains, desert and sheep.

When I couldn't do without alcohol, I drove myself on
    alcohol,
When I couldn't do without cigarettes and coffee, I drove
    myself on cigarettes and coffee.
I was courageous. Industrious. Nearly a model of virtue.
But that is good for nothing.

Please, Doctor, I feel a pain.
Not here. No, not here. Even I don't know.
Maybe it's too many islands and continents,
unpronounced words, bazaars, wooden flutes
or too much drinking to the mirror, without beauty,
though one was to be a kind of archangel
or a Saint George, over there, on St. George Street.

Please, Medicine Man, I feel a pain.
I always believed in spells and incantations.
Sure, women have only one, Catholic, soul,
but we have two. When you start to dance
you visit remote pueblos in your sleep
and even lands you have never seen.

Put on, I beg you, charms made of feathers,
now it's time to help one of your own.
I have read many books but I don't believe them.
When it hurts we return to the banks of certain rivers.
I remember those crosses with chiseled suns and moons
and wizards, how they worked during an outbreak of typhus.
Send your second soul beyond the mountains, beyond time.
Tell me what you saw, I will wait.

TO ROBINSON JEFFERS

If you have not read the Slavic poets
so much the better. There's nothing there
for a Scotch-Irish wanderer to seek. They lived in a childhood
prolonged from age to age. For them, the sun
was a farmer's ruddy face, the moon peeped through a cloud
and the Milky Way gladdened them like a birch-lined road.
They longed for the Kingdom which is always near,
always right at hand. Then, under apple trees
angels in homespun linen will come parting the boughs
and at the white kolkhoz tablecloth
cordiality and affection will feast (falling to the ground at
     times).

And you are from surf-rattled skerries. From the heaths
where burying a warrior they broke his bones
so he could not haunt the living. From the sea night
which your forefathers pulled over themselves, without a
     word.
Above your head no face, neither the sun's nor the moon's
only the throbbing of galaxies, the immutable
violence of new beginnings, of new destruction.

All your life listening to the ocean. Black dinosaurs
wade where a purple zone of phosphorescent weeds
rises and falls on the waves as in a dream. And Agamemnon
sails the boiling deep to the steps of the palace
to have his blood gush onto marble. Till mankind passes
and the pure and stony earth is pounded by the ocean.

Thin-lipped, blue-eyed, without grace or hope,
before God the Terrible, body of the world.

94

Prayers are not heard. Basalt and granite.
Above them, a bird of prey. The only beauty.

What have I to do with you? From footpaths in the orchards,
from an untaught choir and shimmers of a monstrance,
from flower beds of rue, hills by the rivers, books
in which a zealous Lithuanian announced brotherhood, I
    come.
Oh, consolations of mortals, futile creeds.

And yet you did not know what I know. The earth teaches
More than does the nakedness of elements. No one with
    impunity
gives to himself the eyes of a god. So brave, in a void,
you offered sacrifices to demons: there were Wotan and
    Thor,
the screech of Erinyes in the air, the terror of dogs
when Hekate with her retinue of the dead draws near.

Better to carve suns and moons on the joints of crosses
as was done in my district. To birches and firs
give feminine names. To implore protection
against the mute and treacherous might
than to proclaim, as you did, an inhuman thing.

ELEGY FOR N. N.

Tell me if it is too far for you.
You could have run over the small waves of the Baltic
and past the fields of Denmark, past a beech wood
could have turned towards the ocean, and there, very soon
Labrador, white at this season.
And if you, who dreamed about a lonely island,
were frightened of cities and of lights flashing along the
        highway
you had a path straight through the wilderness
over blue-black, melting waters, with tracks of deer and
        caribou
as far as the Sierra and abandoned gold mines.
The Sacramento River could have led you
between hills overgrown with prickly oaks.
Then just a eucalyptus grove, and you had found me.

True, when the manzanita is in bloom
and the bay is clear on spring mornings
I think reluctantly of the house between the lakes
and of nets drawn in beneath the Lithuanian sky.
The bath cabin where you used to leave your dress
has changed forever into an abstract crystal.
Honey-like darkness is there, near the veranda
and comic young owls, and the scent of leather.

How could one live at that time, I really can't say.
Styles and dresses flicker, indistinct,
not self-sufficient, tending towards a finale.
Does it matter that we long for things as they are in
        themselves?

The knowledge of fiery years has scorched the horses standing
    at the forge,
the little columns in the market place,
the wooden stairs and the wig of Mama Fliegeltaub.

We learned so much, this you know well:
how, gradually, what could not be taken away
is taken. People, countrysides.
And the heart does not die when one thinks it should,
we smile, there is tea and bread on the table.
And only remorse that we did not love
the poor ashes in Sachsenhausen
with absolute love, beyond human power.

You got used to new, wet winters,
to a villa where the blood of the German owner
was washed from the wall, and he never returned.
I too accepted but what was possible, cities and countries.
One cannot step twice into the same lake
on rotting alder leaves,
breaking a narrow sunstreak.

Guilt, yours and mine? Not a great guilt.
Secrets, yours and mine? Not great secrets.
Not when they bind the jaw with a kerchief, put a little cross
    between the fingers,
and somewhere a dog barks, and the first star flares up.

No, it was not because it was too far
you failed to visit me that day or night.
From year to year it grows in us until it takes hold,
I understood it as you did: indifference.

THEY WILL PLACE THERE TELESCREENS

They will place telescreens there and our life
will be appearing from end to end
with everything we have managed to forget, as it seemed, for
ever
and with dresses of our time, which would be laughable and
piteous
had we not been wearing them because we knew nothing
better.
Armageddon of men and women. It is no use to cry: I loved
them,
every one seemed to me a child, greedy and in want of caresses.
I liked beaches, swimming pools and clinics
for there they were the bone of my bone, the flesh of my flesh.
I pitied them and myself, but this will not protect me.
The word and the thought are over, a shifting of a glass,
an averting of one's eyes, fingers unbuttoning a blouse,
foolishness,
a cheating gesture, contemplation of clouds,
a convenient dispatch: only that.
And what if they march out, tinkling bells
at their ankles, if slowly they enter the flame
which has taken them as well as me? Bite your (if you have
any) fingers
and again look at everything from end to end.

ON THE OTHER SIDE

*Some hells present an appearance like the ruins of houses
and cities after conflagrations, in which infernal spirits dwell
and hide themselves. In the milder hells there is an appear-
ance of rude huts, in some cases contiguous in the form of a
city with lanes and streets.*

EMANUEL SWEDENBORG

Falling, I caught the curtain,
Its velvet was the last thing I could feel on earth
As I slid to the floor, howling: aah! aaah!

To the very end I could not believe that I too must . . .
Like everyone.

Then I trod in wheel-ruts
on an ill-paved road. Wooden shacks,
A lame tenement house in a field of weeds.
Potato-patches fenced in with barbed wire.
They played as-if-cards, I smelled as-if-cabbage,
There was as-if-vodka, as-if-dirt, as-if-time.
I said: "See here . . . ," but they shrugged their shoulders,
Or averted their eyes. This land knew nothing of surprise.
Nor of flowers. Dry geraniums in tin cans,
A deception of greenery coated with sticky dust.
Nor of the future. Gramophones played, .
Repeating endlessly things which had never been.
Conversations repeated things which had never been.
So that no one should guess where he was, or why.
I saw hungry dogs lengthening and shortening their muzzles,

And changing from mongrels, to greyhounds, then dachshunds,
As if to signify they were perhaps not quite dogs.
Huge flocks of crows, freezing in mid-air,
Exploded under the clouds . . .

BOBO'S METAMORPHOSIS

The distance between being and nothingness is infinite.

("Zabawy przyjemne i pożyteczne" ["*Entertainments pleasant and useful*"], *1776*)

I

Fields sloping down and a trumpet.

*

Dusk and a bird flies low and waters flare.

*

Sails unfurled to the daybreak beyond the straits.

*

I was entering the interior of a lily by a bridge of brocade.

*

Life was given but unattainable.

*

From childhood till old age ecstasy at sunrise.

II

As life goes, many of these mornings.
My eyes closed, I was grown up and small.
I was wearing plumes, silks, ruffles and armor,
Women's dresses, I was licking the rouge.
I was hovering at each flower from the day of creation,
I knocked on the closed doors of the beaver's halls and the
    mole's.
It's incredible that there were so many unrecorded voices
Between a toothpaste and a rusted blade,
Just over my table in Wilno, Warsaw, Brie, Montgeron,
    California.
It's incredible that I die before I attain.

III

From the taste and scent of bird-cherry trees above rivers
Consciousness hikes through bay and hibiscus thickets
Gathering specimens of the Earth into a green box.
Above it, the red bark of *sequoia sempervirens*
And jays, different from those beyond the Bering Straits,
Open their wings of indigo color.
Consciousness alone, without friends and foes,
embraces forest slopes, an eagle's nest.
Incomprehensible as it is to a snake with a yellow stripe,
Itself unable to grasp the principle of the snake and tree.

IV

Stars of Philemon, stars of Baucis,
Above their house entangled by the roots of an oak.
And a wandering god, soundly asleep on a thong-strung bed,
His fist for a pillow.
An advancing weevil encounters his sandal
And pushes on painfully through a foot-polished mesa.

I hear also sounds of a pianoforte.
I steal through humid blackness under the jungle of spirea
Where are scattered clay flasks from Dutch aquavit.
She appears, a young lady with a curl on her ear.
But I grew a beard when walking on all fours
And my Indian bow rotted from snow and rain.
She plays music and simultaneously grows small, sits down
        on her chamberpot,
At a swing she pulls up her skirt
To do indecent things with me or her cousin.
And all of a sudden she walks grayhaired in a scraggy suburb,
Then departs without delay where all the maidens go.

Let there be an island—and an island crops out of the deep.
The pale rose of its cliffs is tinged with violet.
Seeds sprout, on the hills, presto, chestnuts and cedars,
A spring waves a fern just above the harbor.

On flat rocks over fir-green water of the cove
Spirits lounge, similar to skin divers with their oxygen tanks.
The only daughter of a sorcerer, Miranda,
Rides a donkey in the direction of the grotto
By a path strewn with creaking leaves.
She sees a tripod, a kettle, and bundles of dry twigs.
Vanish, island! Or stronger: go away!

V

I liked him as he did not look for an ideal object.
When he heard: "only the object which does not exist
Is perfect and pure," he blushed and turned away.

In every pocket he carried pencils, pads of paper
Together with crumbs of bread, the accidents of life.

Year after year he circled a thick tree
Shading his eyes with his hand and muttering in amazement.

How much he envied those who draw a tree with one line!
But metaphor seemed to him something indecent.

He would leave symbols to the proud busy with their cause.
By looking he wanted to draw the name from the very thing.

When he was old, he tugged at his tobacco-stained beard:
"I prefer to lose thus than to win as they do."

Like Peter Breughel the father he fell suddenly
While attempting to look back between his spread-apart legs.

And still the tree stood there, unattainable.
O veritable, o true to the very core. It was.

VI

They reproached him with marrying one woman and living
    with another.
Have no time—he answered—for nonsense, a divorce and
    so on.
A man gets up, a few strokes of a brush and then already
    it's evening.

VII

Bobo, a nasty boy, was changed into a fly.
In accordance with the rite of the flies he washed himself by a
    rock of sugar
And ran vertically in caves of cheese.
He flew through a window into the bright garden.
There, indomitable ferryboats of leaves
Carried a drop taut with the excess of its rainbow,
Mossy parks grew by ponds of light in the mountains of bark,
An acrid dust was falling from flexible columns inside
    cinnabar flowers.
And though it did not last longer than from teatime till
    supper,
Later on, when he had pressed trousers and a trimmed
    moustache,
He always thought, holding a glass of liquor, that he was
    cheating them
For a fly should not discuss the nation and productivity.
A woman facing him was a volcanic peak
Where there were ravines, craters and in hollows of lava
The movement of earth was tilting crooked trunks of pines.

VIII

Between her and me there was a table, on the table a glass.
The chapped skin of her elbows touched the shining surface
In which the contour of shade under her armpit was reflected.
A drop of sweat thickened over her wavy lip.
And the space between her and me fractionized itself
    infinitely
Buzzing with pennate Eleatic arrows.
Not a year, not a hundred years of journey would exhaust it.
Had I overturned the table what would we have
    accomplished.
That act, a non-act, always no more than potential
Like the attempt to penetrate water, wood, minerals.
But she, too, looked at me as if I were a ring of Saturn
And knew I was aware that no one attains.
Thus were affirmed humanness, tenderness.

OECONOMIA DIVINA

I did not expect to live in such an unusual moment.
When the God of thunders and of rocky heights,
The Lord of hosts, Kyrios Sabaoth,
Would humble people to the quick,
allowing them to act whatever way they wished,
leaving to them conclusions, saying nothing.
It was a spectacle that was indeed unlike
the agelong cycle of royal tragedies.
Roads on concrete pillars, cities of glass and cast-iron,
airfields larger than tribal dominions,
suddenly ran short of their principle and disintegrated.
Not in a dream but really, for, from themselves subtracted,
they could only hold on as do things which should not last.
Out of trees, field stones, even lemons on the table
materiality escaped and their spectrum
proved to be a void, a haze on a film.
Dispossessed of its objects, space was swarming.
Everywhere was nowhere and nowhere, everywhere.
Letters in books turned silver-pale, wobbled and faded.
The hand was not able to trace the palm sign, the river sign,
    or the sign of ibis.
A hullabaloo of many tongues proclaimed the mortality of the
    language.
A complaint was forbidden as it complained to itself.
People, afflicted with an incomprehensible distress,
were throwing off their clothes on the piazzas so that
    nakedness might call for trial.
But in vain they were longing after horror, pity and anger.
Both work and leisure
Were not justified enough,
nor the face, nor the hair nor the loins
nor any existence.

FLIGHT

When we were leaving the burning city,
On the first field path, turning back our eyes,
I said: "Let the grass cover our footprints.
Let the harsh prophets be silent in the fire
And let the dead tell the dead what happened.
We are intended to give birth to a new, violent tribe
Free from the evil and happiness drowsing there.
Let us go—" and a sword of fire opened the earth for us.

HERACLITUS

He pitied them, himself deserving pity.
Because this is beyond the means of any language.
Even his syntax, obscure—as went the reproach—
Words so combined they had triple meaning
Encompassed nothing. Those toes in a sandal,
A girl's breast so fragile under Artemis' hand,
Sweat, oil on the face of a man from the fleet
Participate in the universal, existing separately.
Our own when we are asleep, devoted but to ourselves,
In love with the scent of perishable flesh,
With the central warmth under the pubic hair,
Our knees under our chin, we know there is the All
And we long in vain. An animal's: that is our own.
Particular existence keeps us from the light
(That sentence can be read in reverse as well).
"Nobody was so proud and scornful as he."
For he tortured himself, unable to forgive
That a moment of consciousness never will change us.
Pity turned into anger. So he fled from Ephesus.
Didn't want to see a human face. Lived in the mountains.
Ate grass and leaves, as reports Laertius.
The sea lay down waves beneath the steep shore of Asia
(From above the waves are not seen, you look just at the sea).
And there, is it an echo of bells tinkling at a monstrance?
Or Orlando Furioso's golden clothes afloat?
Or is it a fish's mouth nibbling lipstick
From the lips of a radio-girl drowned in a submarine?

COUNSELS

If I were in the place of young poets
(quite a place, whatever the generation might think)
I would prefer not to say that the earth is a madman's dream,
a stupid tale full of sound and fury.

It's true, I did not happen to see the triumph of justice.
The lips of the innocent make no claims.
And who knows whether a fool in a crown,
a wine cup in his hand, roaring that God favors him
because he poisoned, slew and blinded so many,
would not move the onlookers to tears: he was so gentle.

God does not multiply sheep and camels for the virtuous
and takes nothing away for murder and perjury.
He has been hiding so long that it has been forgotten
how he revealed himself in the burning bush
and in the breast of a young Jew
ready to suffer for all who were and will be.

It is not certain if Ananke awaits her hour
to pay back what is due for the lack of measure and for pride.

Man has been given to understand
that he lives only by the grace of those in power.
Let him therefore busy himself sipping coffee, catching
        butterflies.
Who cares for the Republic will have his right hand cut off.

And yet, the earth merits a bit, a tiny bit, of affection.
Not that I take too seriously consolations of nature,
and baroque ornaments, the moon, chubby clouds

(although it's beautiful when bird-cherries blossom on the
    banks of the Wilia).
No, I would even advise to keep farther from nature,
from persistent images of infinite space,
of infinite time, from snails poisoned
on a path in a garden, just like our armies.

There is so much death, and that is why affection
for pigtails, bright-colored skirts in the wind,
for paper boats no more durable than we are . . .

ON ANGELS

All was taken away from you: white dresses,
wings, even existence.
Yet I believe you,
messengers.

There, where the world is turned inside out,
a heavy fabric embroidered with stars and beasts,
you stroll, inspecting the trustworthy seams.

Short is your stay here:
now and then at a matinal hour, if the sky is clear,
in a melody repeated by a bird,
or in the smell of apples at the close of day
when the light makes the orchards magic.

They say somebody has invented you
but to me this does not sound convincing
for humans invented themselves as well.

The voice—no doubt it is a valid proof,
as it can belong only to radiant creatures,
weightless and winged (after all, why not?),
girdled with the lightning.

I have heard that voice many a time when asleep
and, what is strange, I understood more or less
an order or an appeal in an unearthly tongue:

day draws near
another one
do what you can.

THE MASTER

They say that my music is angelic.
That when the Prince listens to it
His face, hidden from sight, turns gentle.
With a beggar he would share power.
A fan of a lady-in-waiting is immobile,
Silk by its touch does not induce pleasant immodest thoughts
And under a pleat her knees, far off in a chasm, grow numb.

Everyone has heard in the cathedral my Missa Solemnis.
I changed the throats of girls from the Saint Cecilia choir
Into an instrument which raises us
Above what we are. I know how to free
Men and women from remembrances of their long lives
So that they stand in the smoke of the nave
Restored to the mornings of childhood
When a drop of dew and a shout on the mountains
Were the truth of the world.

Leaning on a cane at sunset
I may resemble a gardener
Who has planted and reared a tall tree.

I was not wasting the years of frail youthful hope.
I measure what is done. Over there a swallow
Will pass away and return, changed in its slanting flight.
Steps will be heard at the well but of other people.
The ploughs will erase a forest. The flute and the violin
Will always work as I have ordered them.

No one knows how I was paying. Ridiculous, they believe
It may be got for nothing. We are pierced by a ray.

They want a ray because this helps them to admire.
Or they accept a folk tale: once, under an alder
A demon appeared to us, as black as a pond,
He drew two drops of blood with a sting of a gnat
And impressed in the wax his amethyst ring.

The celestial spheres endlessly resound.
But an instant is invincible in memory.
It comes back in the middle of the night. Who are those
     holding torches,
So that what is long past occurs in full light?

Regret, to no end, in every hour
Of a long life. What beautiful work
Will redeem the heartbeats of a living creature
And what use to confess deeds that last for ever?

When old and white-haired under their laced shawls
They dip their fingers in a basin at the entrance
It seems to me she might have been one of them. The same firs
Rustle and with a shallow wave sheens the lake.

And yet I loved my destiny.
Could I move back time, I am unable to guess
Whether I would have chosen virtue. My line of fate does
     not tell.
Does God really want us to lose our soul
For only then He may receive a gift without blemish?

A language of angels! Before you mention Grace
Mind that you do not deceive yourself and others.
What comes from my evil—that only is true.

DITHYRAMB

We have seen so much on earth and yet malachite mountains
    at sunset are greeted as always with a song and a low bow.
The same spring dance summons when under the rubble of
    basalt cliffs flocks of birds plunge in translucent waters
    of coves.
And a finny hand of a sea otter glimmers as it wallows in the
    foam at Point Lobos.
While in the fog the red of azaleas glows from the bottom
    of steamy ravines.
Nothing has been added, nothing has been taken away,
    o imperturbable, perfect, inviolable world.
No memory is preserved about anything that would be ours
    for certain.
A melody of a mouth organ from afar, from indefinite years
    or a path on which we fell united by a kiss.
Flax asleep on spinning wheels, apples and grain in barn bays,
    brown circles on the breasts of cousin Tonia.
Submachine gun bursts on a plain burrowed with anti-tank
    trenches, under the torn curtain of a cloudy dawn.
Who will affirm, who will call "mine" a fruitless, fruitless,
    painfully called back dream?
With rustling of Renaissance dresses our dead women pass by,
    turn about and put a finger to their lips.
Armored companions sat down at a chessboard, setting aside
    their visored helmets.
And love's dominion, a live gold in blood, annihilates forever
    our empty name.

WHITENESS

O white, white, white. White city where women carry bread
   and vegetables, women born under the signs of the
   ever-gyrating zodiacs.
The jaws of fountains spout water in the green sun as in the
   days past of nuptials, of strolls in the cold aurora from
   one outskirt to another.
Buckles from schoolboys' belts somewhere in the dense earth,
   bunkers and sarcophagi bound with blackberry ropes.
Revelations of touch, again and again new beginnings, no
   knowledge, no memory ever accepted.
A faltering passerby, I walk through a street market after the
   loss of speech.
The candlesticks in the conquerors' tents overflow with wax,
   anger has left me and on my tongue the sourness of
   winter apples.
Two gypsy women rising from the ashes beat a little drum
   and dance for immortal men.
In a sky inhabited or empty (no one cares) just pigeons and
   echoes.
Loud is my lament, for I believed despair could last and love
   could last.
In the white city which does not demand, does not know, does
   not name, but which was and which will be.

THE YEAR

I looked around in the unknown year, aware that few are
    those who come from so far, I was saturated with
    sunlight as a plant with water.
That was a high year, fox-colored, like a crosscut redwood
    stump or vine leaves on the hills in November.
In its groves and chambers the pulse of music was beating
    strongly, running down from dark mountains, tributaries
    entangled.
A generation clad in patterned robes trimmed with little bells
    greeted me with the banging of conga drums.
I repeated their guttural songs of ecstatic despair walking by
    the sea when it bore in boys on surfboards and washed
    my footprints away.
At the very border of inhabited time the same lessons were
    being learned, how to walk on two legs and to pronounce
    the signs traced in the always childish book of our
    species.
I would have related, had I known how, everything which a
    single memory can gather for the praise of men.
O sun, o stars, I was saying, holy, holy, holy, is our being
    beneath heaven and the day and our endless communion.

GIFT

A day so happy.
Fog lifted early, I worked in the garden.
Hummingbirds were stopping over honeysuckle flowers.
There was no thing on earth I wanted to possess.
I knew no one worth my envying him.
Whatever evil I had suffered, I forgot.
To think that once I was the same man did not embarrass me.
In my body I felt no pain.
When straightening up, I saw the blue sea and sails.

WITH TRUMPETS AND ZITHERS

1

The gift was never named. We lived and a hot light created
stood in its sphere.
Castles on rocky spurs, herbs in river valleys, descents into the
bays under ash trees.
All past wars in the flesh, all loves, conch shells of the Celts,
Norman boats by the cliffs.
Breathing in, breathing out, o Elysium, we would kneel and
kiss the earth.
A naked girl crossed a town overgrown with green moss and
bees returned heavy for their evening milking.
Labyrinths of species at our headrest up to the thick of
phosphorous woods at the entrance of limestone caves.
And in a summer rainstorm putting out paper lanterns on
the dark village square, couples laughing in flight.
Water steamed at dawn by Calypso's island where an oriole
flutters in a white crown of a poplar.
I looked at fishermen's dinghies stopped at the other shore and
the year once again turned over, the vintage season
began.

2

I address you, my consciousness, when in a sultry night shot
  with lightnings the plane is landing at Beauvais or
  Kalamazoo.
And a stewardess moves about quietly so not to wake anyone
  while the cellular wax of cities glimmers beneath.
I believed I would understand but it is late and I know
  nothing except laughter and weeping.
The wet grasses of fertile deltas cleaned me from time and
  changed all into a present without beginning or end.
I disappear in architectural spirals, in lines of a crystal, in the
  sound of instruments playing in forests.
Once again I return to excessive orchards and only the echo
  seeks me in that house on the hill under a hundred-year-
  old hazel tree.
Then how can you overtake me, you, weighing blame and
  merit, now when I do not remember who I am and who
  I was?
On many shores at once I am lying cheek on the sand and
  the same ocean runs in, beating its ecstatic drums.

3

And throughout the afternoon the endless talk of cicadas
    while on the slope they are drinking wine from a
    traveler's goblet.
Fingers ripping at meat, juice trickles on graying beards,
    a ring perhaps or glitter of a gold chain round the neck.
A beauty arrives from canopied beds, from cradles on rockers,
    washed and combed by her mother's hand so that
    undoing her hair we remove a tortoise-shell comb.
Skin scented with oils, arch-browed on city squares, her
    breasts for our cupped hands in the Tigris and
    Euphrates gardens.
Then they beat on the strings and shout on the heights and
    below at the bend of a river the campground's orange
    tents slowly surrender to shadows.

4

Nothing but laughter and weeping. Terror and no defense
    and arm in arm they drag me to a pit of tangled bones.
Soon I will join their dance, with bailiffs, wenches and kings,
    such as they used to paint on the tablecloth at our revels.
With a train of my clock carried by the Great Jester, not I,
    just the Sinner to whom a honey-sweet age was brought
    by winged Fortune.
To whom three masked Slavic devils, Duliban, Kostruban,
    Mendrela, squealing and farting, would offer huge
    smoking plates.
Fingers grabbing at fingers, tongues fornicating with tongues,
    but not mine was the sense of touch, not mine was the
    knowledge.
Beyond seven rocky mountains I searched for my Teacher and
    yet I am here, not myself, at a pit of tangled bones.
I am standing on a theatrum, astonished by the last things,
    the puppet Death has black ribs and still I cannot believe.

5

The scent of freshly mown clover redeemed the perished
   armies and the meadows glittered in headlights
   forever.
An immense night of July filled my mouth with a taste of
   rain and near Puybrun by the bridges my childhood
   was given back.
The warm encampments of crickets'chirped under a low
   cloud just as in our lost homelands where a wooden cart
   goes creaking.
Borne by an inscrutable power, one century gone, I heard,
   beating in darkness, the heart of the dead and the living.

6

What separates, falls. Yet my scream "no!" is still heard
   though it burned out in the wind.
Only what separates does not fall. All the rest is beyond
   persistence.
I wanted to describe this, not that, basket of vegetables with
   a redheaded doll of a leek laid across it.
And a stocking on the arm of a chair, a dress crumpled as it
   was, this way, no other.
I wanted to describe her, no one else, asleep on her belly,
   made secure by the warmth of his leg.
Also a cat in the unique tower as purring he composes his
   memorable book.
Not ships but one ship with a blue patch in the corner
   of its sail.
Not streets, for once there was a street with a shop sign:
   "Schuhmacher Pupke."
In vain I tried because what remains is the ever-recurring
   basket.
And not she whose skin perhaps I, of all men, loved,
   but a grammatical form.
No one cares that precisely this cat wrote *The Adventures of
   Telemachus.*
And the street will always be only one of many streets without
   name.

From a limbo for unbaptized infants and for animal souls let
    a dead fox step out to testify against the language.
Standing for a second in an ant-wing light of pine-needles
    before a boy summoned to speak of him forty years later.
Not a general one, a plenipotentiary of the idea of the fox,
    in his cloak lined with the universals.
But he, from a coniferous forest near the village Zegary.
I bring him before the high tribunal in my defense, for what
    remains after desires, are doubt and much regret.
And one runs and sails through archipelagos in the hope of
    finding a place of immutable possession.
Till chandeliers in the rooms of Heloise or Annalena die out
    and angels blow trumpets on the steps of a sculptured
    bed.
A cheerless dawn advances beyond a palm-lined alley, loudly
    proclaimed by the rattling surf.
And whatever once entered a bolted house of the five senses
    now is set in the brocade of the style.
Which, your honor, does not distinguish particular cases.

8

At dawn the expanse takes its rise, a high horizontal whiteness
    up to the slopes of Tamalpais.
It is torn apart and in the wool of vapor a herd of islands and
    promontories on their watery pastures.
Knife-blue in twilight, a rose-tinted tin, liquid copper,
    izumrud, smaragdos.
Quiverfuls of buildings touched by a ray: Oakland, San
    Francisco, before the mica in motion lights up below:
    Berkeley, El Cerrito.
In the oceanic wind eucalyptus husks clashing and
    disentangling.
Height, length and width take in their arms a sleeping
    caterpillar of a rolled body.
And carry it over a frozen waste of the Sierras to the most
    distant province of the continent.
Layers of Christmas tinsels wheel round, cities on the bay,
    buckled by luminous ropes of three bridges.
In the hour of ending night it amazes—this place, this time,
    assigned for an awakening of this particular body.

9

I asked what was the day. It was St. Andrew's Eve.
She and her smashed little mirrors under the weeds and
    snows where also the States and banners molder.
Outlandish districts in mud up to the axle-tree, names I
    alone remember: Gineitai, Apytalakys.
In the silence of stopped spinning-wheels, fear by the flame of
    two candles, a mouse scratching, a nuptial of phantoms.
In electronic music I heard lugubrious sirens, people's
    panicky calls crushed into flutters and rustles.
I was sitting before a mirror but no hand reached out of
    darkness to touch me on the shoulder.
There, behind me, flash after flash, flocks of birds were taking
    off from the banks of spring ice.
Fanning with their four wings storks stood on their nest in
    a majestic copulation.
My dishonest memory did not preserve anything, save the
    triumph of nameless births.
When I would hear a voice, it seemed to me I distinguished
    in it words of forgiveness.

10

The dream shared at night by all people has inhabitants,
 hairy animals.
It is a huge and snug forest and everyone entering it walks
 on all fours till dawn through the very thick of the tangle.
Through the wilderness inaccessible to metal objects,
 all-embracing like a warm and deep river.
In satin tunnels the touch distinguishes apples and their color
 that does not recall anything real.
All are quadrupeds, their thighs rejoice at the badger-bear
 softness, their rosy tongues lick the fur of each other.
The "I" is felt with amazement in the heartbeat, but so
 large it cannot be filled by the whole Earth with her
 seasons.
Nor would the skin guarding a different essence trace any
 boundary.
Later on, in crude light, separated into you and me, they try
 with a bare foot pebbles of the floor.
The two-legged, some to the left, some to the right, put on
 their belts, garters, slacks and sandals.
And they move on their stilts, longing after a forest home,
 after low tunnels, after an assigned return to It.

11

A coelentera, all pulsating flesh, animal-flower,
All fire, made up of falling bodies joined together by the
    black pin of sex.
It breathes in the center of a galaxy, drawing to itself a star
    after a star.
And I, an instant of its duration, on multi-laned roads which
    penetrate half-opened mountains.
Bare mountains overgrown with an ageless grass, opened and
    frozen at a sunset before the generations.
Where at large curves one sees nests of cisterns or transparent
    towers, perhaps of missiles.
Along brown leaks by the sea shore, rusty stones and
    butcheries where quartered whales are ground to powder.
I wanted to be a judge but those whom I called "they" have
    changed into myself.
I was getting rid of my faith so as not to be better than men and
    women who are certain only of their unknowing.
And on the roads of my terrestrial homeland turning round
    with the music of the spheres
I thought that all I could do would be done better one day.

ABOUT THE AUTHOR

Czesław Miłosz was born in Lithuania in 1911. His books of poetry in English include *The Collected Poems, 1931–1987, Unattainable Earth, The Separate Notebooks, Provinces, Bells in Winter,* and *Selected Poems,* all published by The Ecco Press. He is a member of the American Academy and Institute of Arts and Letters and was awarded the Nobel Prize for Literature in 1980.